Guru Nanak

Compiled by Mrs Rungeen Singh

Young Learner Publications ™

G-1 Rattan Jyoti,
18 Rajendra Place,
New Delhi -110008 (INDIA)
Ph.: 25750801, 25820556
Fax: 91-11-25764396

Printed at : Kumar Offset Printers, Delhi-92

CONTENTS

"Guru Nanak Sah fakir
Hindu ka Guru
Musalman ka Pir"

The first Sikh guru, Guru Nanak Dev ji was born on 15th April, 1469. Even as a child, Guru Nanak surprised people with his unusual religious sensibility, his knowledge about divine things and his exceptional tendencies for contemplation. His extraordinary worldly knowledge is evident from the fact that he had learnt Hindi and Sanskrit at the tender age of seven, and Persian at the age of thirteen.

He was an extraordinary poet and a skilled musician. He wrote 947 hymns and composed various tunes in Indian classical ragas that enamoured the heart and soul of all who heard them. These hymns provide the moral and spiritual guidelines for the followers of Sikhism.

It is important to note that Guru Nanak expressed his message in the spoken language of the people of North India, i.e. Punjabi, as opposed to Sanskrit, the language of the elite in which the Hindu vedas are written. This clearly indicates that his message was intended for the masses.

Guru Nanak revolted against false rituals, superstition, caste system, asceticism, idol worship, etc. He supported the cause of women, the poor and the down-trodden, and worked towards social reformation. A major tool of this social reformation was the institution of *langar*, which was established for the benefit of the under-priviledged. This practice of providing free food to the poor and needy also helped to break the boundaries of class, caste and gender.

Guru Nanak preached about a God who is the creator of all things. A God who is Supreme, All-powerful, Formless, Self-existent, Ever-lasting. All-knowing, Omnipotent, Infinite, Eternal, Incomprehensible, All-giver and the Absolute Truth.

Guru Nanak Dev ji was born on 15th April, 1469 in the Western Punjab village of Talwandi (now in Pakistan) about 65 km west of Lahore.

He was born in a simple Hindu family. His family was very happy when he was born. There was a lot of love among his family members.

His mother's name was Tripta and his father's name was Mehta Kalian Das.

His sister's name was Nanki. So his parents named him Nanak. The place where he was born is today called 'Nankana Sahib'.

His father, called Kalu, was the Chief Patwari under the Talwandi ruler Rai Bular.

His family was well to do. There was no lack of money as his father worked for the ruler.

As he grew, he became friends with children of both the Hindu and the Muslim households. One of his much loved childhood companion was Mardana.

THE STARS FORETELL

From the very first day, the family felt that Nanak was a very special boy.

All newborn babies cry when they are born. But it is said that when Nanak was born, he did not cry at all.

Everyone observed his smiling and happy countenance as a baby.

His parents asked the priest to make his horoscope which would tell them about his stars and what would happen to him in life.

The priest told them that Nanak was born under lucky stars. He predicted that he would achieve great heights as a spiritual leader and would reform the world. He would teach the people and make them better human beings.

Nanak's mother was a very religious lady. She taught him that *Sat Kartar* meant that 'God is the only Truth'. That is why even as a child, his favourite chant was *Sat Kartar*.

His mother also taught him not to be selfish and to share his things with others.

So whenever his mother gave him sweets, he distributed them among his friends.

Nanak would sit under a tree with his friends and sing devotional songs.

Once when Nanak was singing with his friends, the Muslim ruler Rai Bular passed through that way. He sat down to listen to the wonderful religious songs sung by the children.

He felt so delighted listening to them that he forgot about the world and just thought of God.

He listened till Nanak and the children finished their singing.

He felt that Nanak was a blessed child. He called Nanak's father, Kalu, and told him that he had heard Nanak sing religious songs near the pond.

He praised the way Nanak sung, with so much faith. It was this faith in the Almighty that lent such sweetness to his voice.

He advised Nanak's father to take good care of Nanak as he was a gifted child.

At the age of five, Nanak was sent to Pandit Gopaldas Pande to study Mathematics and to learn to read and write in Hindi.

Nanak was very quick in learning and very clever in understanding what was taught to him.

Nanak with his inquisitive mind would ask many questions to his teacher and surprise him.

Once when his teacher Pandit Gopaldas Pande was chanting 'Om', Nanak interrupted him politely and asked him what it meant.

The teacher was very surprised that a five-year-old boy wanted to know the meaning of 'Om'.

He told Nanak that 'Om' was the name used for God.

Nanak remarked, "But my mother says that *Sat Kartar* is the name used for God. 'Sat' means truth and *Sat Kartar* means that God is the only Truth."

Then the teacher explained that God had many names out of which two names were *Om* and *Sat Kartar*.

Even at a young age, Nanak showed signs of unusual sensibility by asking questions about God and life.

One day, the teacher went and confessed to Nanak's father, "Your son is a genius. I have taught Nanak all that I know. There is nothing left for me to teach him. Please take him somewhere else to study."

Nanak's learning at such a young age paved the way for what he taught his followers later in his life.

He taught the people that though God was called by many names, like *Ram* and *Allah*, there was only one God.

The people began to believe that the worship by different people in different ways still meant that there was one God.

When the animosity between the Hindus and the Muslims increased, these beliefs helped. Guru Nanak's teachings also helped those people who were suffering because of the unnatural divides constructed by men such as caste, creed, gender, etc.

Guru Nanak taught that all the people were equal and that common people could reach God themselves. They did not need priests as mediators between themselves and God.

Nanak's father, Mehta Kalian, sent Nanak to study Muslim literature and to learn the Persian and Arabic languages.

On the first day, the teacher started teaching Nanak with the first Persian alphabet 'alif'. Nanak at once asked him the meaning of *alif*. The teacher could not explain it to him.

Then Nanak explained to the teacher, "*Alif* means one God. *Alif* stands for Allah which is the Muslim name for God. It is the same as *Om* or *Sat Kartar*."

The teacher was very surprised. He realised that Nanak already knew a lot.

As time passed, he was shocked to see that Nanak's knowledge knew no bounds.

He took Nanak to his father and requested, "Please take back your son. I can't teach him any more."

Mehta Kalian asked, "Why can't you teach my son?"

The teacher said, "Your clever child does not need to be taught anything by me."

"Why doesn't he need to be taught by you? What makes you say that?" asked his father.

Guru Nanak

The teacher admitted, "He knows more than I myself know. He will teach the world. What can I teach him? He knows everything."

In the olden times, there were many rituals which the priests asked the people to perform. The masses did exactly what the priests told them to do. One such ritual was the wearing of a white thread called *janeyu* in a holy ceremony.

The *janeyu* was joined into a long, circular thread and worn over one shoulder, across the chest, dropping at the other side.

When Nanak was nine years old, Mehta Kalian wanted to perform this sacred thread ceremony for him. He invited all his relatives and friends for a grand celebration of the ceremony.

When the priest took the sacred thread to put it around Nanak, Nanak enquired, "Why are you putting this thread around me?"

"It is written in our religious scriptures that the wearing of this sacred thread denotes the second birth as by birth we are all Sudras. It is a sacred ceremony which is being performed for ages by the Brahmins, Kshatriyas and Vaishyas," said the priest.

"Why don't the Sudras get this *janeyu*?" asked Nanak.

"Because our religious books consider them ineligible for that," replied the priest.

"But you just said that by birth we are all Sudras, and it is only after this ceremony that we become a Brahmin, a Kshatriya or a Vaishya. If we are all Sudras, we too must not be allowed to wear this *janeyu*," said Nank.

"This is what is written in the scriptures. Nanak, you must not question the scriptures. It is a sin to do that," said the priest.

"God gave us brain to think and question what is wrong and what is right. There cannot be a sin in using one's intellect. If we don't question, how will we understand?" said Nanak.

The priest had no answer to this. He stood speechless before Nanak and the villagers.

Nanak again asked, "Please tell me why people of different castes wear different *janeyu*? Why don't Sudras, Muslims and women wear *janeyu*? Why do some people wear it and some don't? Why do we wear a thread that divides and discriminates people?"

Nanak continued, "This sacred thread doesn't stop people from lying and

Guru Nanak

committing other serious crimes. If this thread won't make me a better person or bring me closer to God, why should I wear it? If you have a thread that will motivate me to do good deeds then make me wear that thread."

The priest evidently had no answer to Nanak's questions.

All the guests and the villagers realised that what Nanak had said was true. There was no use of a custom that had no meaning.

After Nanak's refusal to perform the ritual, the family members went home without the sacred thread ceremony being performed.

Nanak had both wisdom and courage to challenge such age old customs. Before performing an old custom, he would analyse its worth and wouldn't perform it blindly.

Throughout his life, he taught people not to follow the old customs blindly. He taught them that the mechanical performance of a ritual wouldn't make them close to God.

The priests had made many customs and rituals which were useful for the material well being of their caste, but useless for the spiritual growth of a person.

Nanak wanted such obsolete and meaningless customs to be abolished, and

Guru Nanak

only those old customs to be continued which were beneficial for humanity at large.

According to him only those customs should be followed which gave peace and contentment to the people and were based on the principles of love, truth and equality.

After this incident, Nanak spent much of his time in singing religious songs in the company of holy men.

WORLDLY DUTY

When Mehta Kalian saw his son singing religious songs with holy men, he became worried.

He told his wife, "Nanak has already learnt everything which can be taught here. There is nothing to occupy him. What if he turns into an idler?"

"We should give him something to do, so that he stays busy," advised Nanak's mother Tripta.

"That is what I was thinking too," and then he suggested, "I think I will tell him to look after our cattle while they are grazing."

"Yes, that is a nice idea. It will keep him busy," agreed Tripta.

Mehta Kalian called Nanak and told him to take charge of the cattle from the very next day. As usual Nanak politely obeyed his father.

From the next day, he started taking the cattle for grazing.

Guru Nanak

When he took the cattle for grazing, he took his close Muslim friend Mardana with him.

Nanak would sing songs praising God, and Mardana would play the rubab, a musical instrument that Nanak had lent him.

THE SNAKE HOOD

One day when Nanak took his cattle for grazing, he sat thinking about God as *Sat Kartar* and fell asleep.

On seeing Nanak sleeping, Mardana drove the cattle into another field because he did not want Nanak to be disturbed.

Nanak was now alone while he was sleeping. The rays of the sun were falling right on his face.

Suddenly a white serpent appeared. The ruler Rai Bular was passing from that way, and he saw the serpent near Nanak.

He thought he should go and prevent the serpent from biting Nanak. But then he saw that the serpent went and spread his hood.

The serpent lay near Nanak's head and held its huge hood in such a way that there was shade on Nanak's face.

The serpent was shielding Nanak from the harsh sunlight.

Guru Nanak

Rai Bular was amazed to see that the serpent was giving shade to Nanak instead of biting him.

When he went home, he told his servant, "Go quickly and find out who that boy was. That boy will either grow up to be a great king or a great saint. What I have seen today is the most unusual thing to happen."

Rai Bular could not stop himself from telling the people at his court about what he had seen. He said, "Today I'll tell you of a very strange thing I saw."

The courtiers were amazed to hear of a serpent protecting a sleeping boy from the harsh rays of the sun, as this was something unheard of.

Most of them agreed that this could only happen to a special person; a person of high spiritual status. Now, along with Rai Bular, the courtiers were also eager to know who that boy was.

The servant returned and told Rai Bular, "My Lord, that boy is called Nanak. He is the son of Mehta Kalu, who works for you as a Chief Patwari. Today when you saw him in the field, he had come there for grazing his cattle."

Guru Nanak

The servant further said that Nanak was a wise boy who believed in *Sat Kartar*. The king then expressed his wish to meet Nanak some day.

THE CROPS

Nanak daily took the cattle to the fields. One day he dozed off and the cows went into the nearby fields.

The farmers were not there, and the cows ate a lot of their crops.

Many birds also came and started eating the grains from the fields. When Nanak woke up and saw this, he thought of God, who had made ways for everyone to live.

Nanak and Mardana did not stop the birds from eating the crops.

Nanak felt that the crops belonged to God and the birds belonged to God. So why should they be stopped from eating the crops.

The farmers came and saw that the cattle and the birds were eating their crops. They were angry with Nanak and Mardana for not stopping their cattle from destroying the crops.

Guru Nanak

When the farmers started beating the cattle to drive them away from their farms, the soft-hearted Nanak could not bear to see this.

He told his friend Mardana, "Please go and stop the farmers from beating the cattle. I cannot bear to see them being beaten."

Mardana and Nanak tried to stop the farmers from hurting the cattle, but the farmers just didn't listen to them; they were very angry at their loss.

One farmer shouted at Nanak, "First you let the cows spoil our fields and then you don't let us drive them away."

Another farmer said, "You should be punished for this. I will tell Rai Bular to take money from your father for the loss we have incurred."

Nanak replied, "You can complain to him, but don't beat the poor and innocent cattle. They do not know that they have done something wrong."

The farmers went to Rai Bular and told him of how Mehta Kalian's cattle had destroyed and eaten up their crops.

The farmers wanted that Nanak's father should pay money for the loss they had to suffer because of his cattle.

Guru Nanak

Rai Bular patiently listened to the complaints of the angry farmers.

He then called Mehta Kalian and told him that he would have to pay the farmers for their loss.

When Nanak came to know about this, he told the farmers, "Please harvest your crop and sell it first."

"How will that help?" asked one of the farmers.

Nanak said, "If the money you get from its sale is less than before, then we will pay you."

"Half our crops have been lost. We would hardly make any money this time," said one of the farmers.

However, Nanak convinced the farmers to harvest their crops and sell it in the market before taking money from Mehta Kalian.

When they sold their crops, they realised that though a lot of their crops had been eaten by the birds and the cattle, they still had made more profit than ever before.

The farmers were very surprised at the unexpected profit they had made.

Guru Nanak

They thought that this must be because of Nanak's powers.

The farmers told Nanak him about their profit and asked forgiveness for their harsh attitude.

Nanak replied, "Who am I to forgive anyone? Ask *Sat Kartar* for forgiveness."

The farmers became his followers and from that day they followed all his teachings. They started trusting Nanak as a special person with qualities of a saint.

A lot of people became his followers when they saw his greatness.

Many poor people too became his followers when Nanak said that even the poor should be respected.

Nanak's name and fame spread far and wide as people came to recognise him as one who enlightened the way to God through his wisdom.

Until this moment, only the priests had control over religion and God. The common man thought that they could not approach God directly. But now Nanak taught that everyone, even the low caste people, could worship God.

Nanak said that any human being could communicate with God directly. His revolutionary ideas made many people his followers, and offended others.

NANAK GETS AN ANSWER

After this incident, Nanak became very moody and sad. He would often get lost in deep thinking.

At times, he would not take the cattle out for grazing but would just sit and think.

His mother and father noticed this change in Nanak. One day his parents tried to get him out of his sad and contemplative mood.

When he didn't cheer up, his parents got more worried and thought that something had happened to Nanak.

They called a doctor to check Nanak. When the doctor came, Nanak told him, "You will not be able to help me."

"Let me try," said the doctor.

Nanak refused, "You won't understand my pain. It's not the body, it's my mind. You can go."

The doctor asked, "If I go, who will help you?"

Guru Nanak

Nanak calmly said, "Whoever has given me the pain will get me out of this too."

Slowly he nodded his head and stated, "Yes I have got the cure now."

His father asked, "What is it Nanak?"

Nanak replied with conviction, "I should leave everything in the hands of God."

Then he smiled as if he had got the answer and the cure to his problem.

Soon he became normal again and started staying cheerful.

His parents realised that their son was not an ordinary boy. He was special and was among the few who meditate and contemplate on things beyond the world. But because Nanak was their only son, they would often get worried about his future.

His mother was patient and understanding towards him and accepted Nanak's meditative mood as a sign of his connection with God.

TRUE BARGAIN

Mehta Kalian wanted to bind Nanak to worldly affairs. He felt that his son Nanak was now old enough to earn some money.

One day, he gave Nanak twenty rupees and told him to go and strike a profitable bargain in the market with that money.

Nanak went to the market with his friend, Bala. On their way, they saw some very poor hermits sitting.

Nanak felt very sorry for the weak and hungry hermits, who didn't even have proper clothes to wear.

Nanak had always been a kind person. As the sufferings of other people greatly pained him, he could not stop himself from spending the money his father had given him, to help those poor hermits.

He went to the market with Bala and spent all the money his father had given him to buy food and clothes for the poor hermits.

Then he distributed the food and the clothes among the poor and hungry hermits.

When he had helped the poor, he felt as if it was the best business or deal he

could have made. He felt that no transaction could be more profitable for his life.

However, on reaching home, Nanak's father asked him, "Nanak, how much profit have you made with the money I gave you?"

When Nanak told his father that he had spent the money on food and clothes and had given them to the poor hermits, his father was very angry.

Mehta Kalian shouted at his son, "How could you spend all my hard earned money on the hermits!"

He was about to treat Nanak harshly but Nanki intervened on Nanak's behalf. She strongly defended Nanak's noble deed.

Nanak's sister Nanki and her husband Jai Ram had come home for a visit. Because of them, his father did not punish Nanak.

Rai Bular had always liked Nanak. When he heard about this incident, he called Nanki and her husband Jai Ram to meet him at his palace.

When they came to meet him, he told Jai Ram to take Nanak with him to Sultanpur. Jai Ram agreed as he cared about Nanak.

Rai Bular also called Mehta Kalian to his palace. He told him, "Take these twenty rupees. This is the amount of money that you gave Nanak and he spent them on the poor hermits. Take it and keep it."

When Nanak's father asked why he was giving it, Rai Bular replied, "I have heard that you scolded Nanak."

Mehta Kalian admitted, "Yes, My Lord. I did scold Nanak."

Rai Bular answered, "Now promise me that you will not scold him. Nanak is like my son. Don't scold him ever again. If he causes you any loss, then I will compensate you for that loss. Your son is God's own child. Just let him do what he likes."

From that day Mehta Kalian did not scold his son, Nanak. He let him do whatever he wanted.

BOUNDLESS KNOWLEDGE

One day Mehta and Pandit Gopaldas saw Nanak reading the *Bhagwad Gita*. They also sat down with him.

When the priest asked Nanak what he knew about the book, Nanak recited the entire *Gita* without looking at the book at all.

Then he told them that the main teaching of the *Gita* was to show that God is the highest knowledge, and it is God who controls life and nature.

He also told them that what is important is the soul and not the body. The greatest truth is that human beings get rewards or punishments according to their actions; good or bad.

Both the priest and Nanak's father were surprised at Nanak's knowledge of the *Gita*.

Mehta Kalian remembered how quickly Nanak had learnt everything from his teachers.

He knew that Nanak loved to recite devotional songs with holy men and at times he would become sad and contemplative.

He had heard about the snake shading him with his hood.

Thinking about these things, he became worried that Nanak might leave them to become a holy man. He might want to be away from worldly things and leave the house as ascetics do.

Guru Nanak

He decided to ask Jai Ram and Nanki to take Nanak to Sultanpur with them.

He thought that this change of place might bring about a change in his son, attaching him to worldly affairs.

When he spoke to them about it, they readily agreed to take Nanak with them, as they had already been asked by Rai Bular to do so.

One day, Nanki suggested, "Why don't we get Nanak married? Once he will have a wife, he will earn money and become responsible."

Everyone felt that it was a good idea to get Nanak married. But now they would have to search for a bride.

Nanki had a girl in mind. She said, "Moolchand's daughter Sulakhni would be a good match for Nanak."

When Nanki asked Nanak if he was ready for marriage, he refused. But as they persisted, he finally agreed.

Mehta Kalu felt that this sweet girl would make Nanak practical and change him into a man of the world.

The proposal of marriage between Sulakhni and Nanak was discussed, and both the families agreed.

So in 1485, when Nanak was sixteen, he was married to Sulakhni.

It was a very simple wedding, as Nanak did not want a grand wedding.

Nanak refused to have any old fashioned customs or any rituals of worship in the marriage. He said that any time was auspicious for the marriage. He also resisted against the matching of horoscopes.

Nanak simply went around the holy fire with his bride Sulakhni and took the oath of marriage in the name of God.

The family members were very happy at Nanak's marriage. They gave their blessings and best wishes to the couple.

Nanak's family thought that Sulakhni would make him feel like a family man with duties.

They thought that now Nanak would not want to renounce the world and go away alone as an ascetic.

Nanak's companion, Mardana, came to the wedding and wished the couple a happy married life.

He asked him, "Brother, what gift will you give me so that I remember this day?"

Nanak gave him his rubab which he used to lend him to play while Nanak sang.

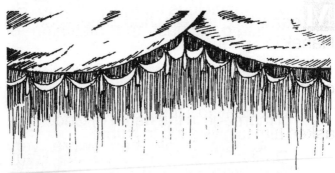

Meanwhile, Jai Ram had found a job for Nanak in Sultanpur.

Jai Ram had been working in the court of Daulat Khan Lodi.

He went to Daulat Khan Lodi and asked him to give a job to Nanak.

Daulat Khan Lodi liked Jai Ram because he was a gentle and honest person.

He knew that Jai Ram would only bring honest and deserving people for jobs.

On Jai Ram's recommendation, Nanak was at once taken as a storekeeper in Sultanpur.

He had to look after the state granary. Nanak took his job very seriously.

He would wake up early in the morning. After taking his bath he would say his prayers and would then go for his work, and return late at night after a hard day's work.

Jai Ram and Nanki were very happy to see Nanak working so well in the state granary.

Nanak stayed with his sister Nanki and her husband Jai Ram in the beginning. They all happily lived together because they loved and respected each other a lot.

Nanak continued living in Sultanpur with his wife, and there they had their two sons.

His son Sri Chand was born in 1494 and Lakshmi Chand in 1497.

Nanak worked in the state granary under the Muslim ruler of Sultanpur, Daulat Khan Lodi, for twelve years.

Nanak was very honest and good. But he did not keep any account of what was stored in the granary.

He gave people whatever they wanted from the granary. He made no difference between people of different religions or castes.

Many poor people started coming to him, and he would give everyone whatever they asked for.

The poor people loved Nanak for his kindness, and he became famous as Nanak Dev.

In the store, he would count out one, two, three till thirteen, and then he would stop.

He just wouldn't count after that and people could take any amount above that.

At times people laughed at Nanak that he did not know how to count beyond thirteen, but the fact was something else.

In Hindi, thirteen is called 'tera' which also means 'yours'. 'Tera' would remind him that everything belonged to God. He thought that if everything belonged to God who was he to prevent it from being given to God's own children. The grains belonged to God, and if God wanted to give it to the poor who was he to stop them.

So he distributed all the amounts above thirteen without counting. For him it was like following an order of his *Sat Kartar*.

There was no cheating in this for him. He was very honest about it; moreover, he never kept it for himself but gave it to the poor and the needy.

Along with fulfilling his worldly duties, Nanak continued to compose and sing devotional songs.

Mardana would play the rubab and his other childhood friend Bala would play the small flat drum while they sang God's praises.

There were many people who were jealous of Nanak's growing fame.

They wanted to spoil Nanak's reputation in the eyes of the courtiers and Nanak's followers. So they went to Daulat Khan Lodi to complain against Nanak.

They tried to turn Daulat Khan against Nanak by telling him that he was trying to empty the state granary.

They complained, "Nanak is giving away everything from the granary. If he continues doing this, your state will have nothing left."

Daulat Khan Lodi gave an order to an accountant to check the stocks of the granary.

Along with the accountant, he sent Jai Ram and the people who complained against Nanak to the granary. All these people together checked the accounts because Lodi wanted to give a fair chance to everybody.

When they had checked everything, they came and told Daulat Khan that everything in the granary was in order. Nanak had not cheated at all.

This was indeed a miracle. God had saved his devotee by ensuring that the granary was full.

The people who had complained against Nanak were afraid that now Daulat Khan would punish them.

Guru Nanak

Daulat Khan was indeed very angry, but he did not punish them. He let them off with a warning.

He told Nanak that those people had not lessened his trust in Nanak.

But this incident had a strong effect on Nanak. It strengthened Nanak's faith in his *Sat Kartar*.

Nanak, who found reasons to contemplate God in everything around him (even in an arithmetical number 'tera') was rescued by God Himself from all possible problems.

NANAK RETURNS

Early one morning, Nanak went to bathe in the River Beas with his companion, Mardana.

Mardana came out of the river to wash his clothes. He saw Nanak bathing in the river.

When he saw that Nanak was going towards the middle of the river, he shouted out, "Be careful! The river is deep there!"

Mardana saw Nanak take a dip, but he did not come out of the river water. He got very scared and worried when Nanak did not come out for a long time. He started looking for him.

At home, Sulakhni was waiting for Nanak to come back home, but he didn't return. Nanki went to Sulakhni and found out that Nanak had not returned.

Everyone was worried. They sent out a search party. They searched everywhere, but Nanak was not to be found.

People said, "Nanak must have drowned in the river."

The whole family was in tears. Even the people in the city and the court came running to find out about Nanak.

When Nanak did not return for two days, everyone thought that probably Nanak was dead.

But Nanki cried, "My brother is a holy soul. He cannot die like this."

Every day Mardana would go to the place where Nanak had drowned. On the third day, Mardana was shocked to see Nanak sitting under the tree, where they had often sat singing hymns.

Mardana fell at his feet and cried with joy. Then he ran all over the city shouting, "Nanak is alive! He has come back!"

Everyone in his family was overjoyed to see him safe and alive.

Nanak had become so popular that nearly everyone in the city started running towards him when they heard that he was alive.

They felt very happy to see him sitting alive and safe under the tree, just as he sat before.

All the people sat around Nanak. He was no longer the same person he had been. There was a divine glow on his face. He seemed as if he was in a trance. The first thing he said was, "There is no Hindu, no Muslim."

They asked, "Where had you been for the past three days, Nanak?"

Nanak replied, "I met my *Sat Kartar*."

"Did you really meet God?" they asked.

Nanak answered, "Yes, I met the Immortal Lord, my *Sat Kartar*, who is truly glorious and sublime."

"But how could you see God?" questioned the people.

"A true devotee can see God. God is truth. God has divine light," stated Nanak.

Nanak told them that God had commanded him to go out in the world and teach people.

When Nanak came home, Nanki took him in her arms. She cried, "Where did you go? We were so worried about you."

Nanak told Nanki about his contact with God and the orders God had given.

Nanak is said to have gone to the state granary after this.

It is said that he opened the doors of the granary and allowed the people to take away whatever they wanted.

Few men ran to Daulat Khan to tell him that the people were looting the state granary. They blamed Nanak for it.

However, when things were checked, they found that the stock was intact and the accounts were correct.

This time Daulat Khan was very angry at the people who were again blaming Nanak for something he had not done.

When he asked Nanak to take charge of the granary again, he refused saying that now he had to fulfill his spiritual duty.

He had started on the path of God, and now he spent all his time teaching people about God and how to live a morally good life.

Nanak would sit under a tree and preach the word of God to the people.

He preached that people should live with love and tolerance towards each other. He spread the message of brotherhood and equality.

He also taught that one should love the other person as oneself. One should even love one's enemies.

He did not hate even the people who had complained against him to Daulat Khan.

Nanak himself did not think of anyone as his enemy, and if they did something to hurt him, he responded with love.

Nanak preached that there were no Hindus or Muslims. Everyone was equal.

When Daulat Khan heard these teachings, he didn't like it. He called Nanak and asked him whether he was a Hindu or a Muslim.

Nanak said, "I am neither a Hindu nor a Muslim. I am a man of God."

When Daulat Khan asked him if he would pray with them in a mosque, Nanak agreed. He went with him to a mosque.

Daulat Khan and the *Qazi* (the chief priest) with him started their prayers called *namaz*. Everyone bent over to pray, but Nanak remained standing.

Daulat Khan asked Nanak, "Why don't you pray with us?"

Nanak said, "You all are not praying properly. You are only praying outwardly. Inwardly you are thinking of other things. What is the use of such prayer?"

"What was I thinking of?" questioned the *Qazi*.

"You were thinking of your new colt," Nanak answered.

The *Qazi* was really surprised. It was true that he had been thinking of his colt. He wondered how Nanak had known this.

"What was I thinking?" questioned Daulat Khan.

Nanak replied, "You were thinking about buying horses."

Daulat Khan admitted, "You are right! I was thinking about buying horses."

Daulat Khan and the *Qazi* now felt that Nanak had true knowledge and was a great man because he could even read the innermost thoughts of people.

Nanak explained to both of them that true worship is a matter of sincere devotion and not religious formality.

They fell at Nanak's feet and exclaimed, "You are truly God's man."

They picked up Nanak and carried him on their shoulders. Soon people from various places came to visit Guru Nanak.

The Hindus and the Muslims were together in the same procession praising Guru Nanak.

Everyone thought of Nanak as a *guru* or teacher, but Nanak felt that he himself needed a guru. So he let himself be a disciple of *Sat Kartar* and let God decide his path for him.

He felt that there were many evil customs in society which had to be removed.

He yearned to make a society which gave equal respect to all.

He wanted all the people to live with love in a state of peace and happiness. So he taught them to love each other and practice religious tolerance.

Nanak was now called *Guru Nanak Dev* by his followers.

In the evenings Mardana and Bala would join Guru Nanak, and they would sing the praises of God.

Guru Nanak told Mardana that to spread God's message over other countries he would have to travel.

Mardana told Guru Nanak that he would accompany him wherever he went. He stayed with Guru Nanak till the end of his life.

Guru Nanak and Mardana decided to leave Sultanpur and travel abroad to spread God's words.

When Guru Nanak told his family that he would leave them, they were all very upset.

His mother cried, "You are our only son. Who will look after us in our old age when you go away?"

His father asked, "What about your duty towards your wife and family?"

Sulakhni's parents were also worried about their daughter.

Guru Nanak answered, "God has told me to preach people and bring them close to Him. He will look after all of you."

Nanki asked, with tears in her eyes, "What will we do when we need you?"

Guru Nanak told them, "I will always be there for you in spirit. Whenever you need me, I will come to you. But I have to go to do what *Sat Kartar* has told me to do. That is my duty."

The family tried to stop Nanak from going, but Nanak had made up his mind.

Guru Nanak declared, "Now worldly relationships can't hold me. I have to fulfill my duties towards God."

His family knew that Nanak was not an ordinary man. They had understood that Nanak was the chosen man of God.

They knew that he was not just for his own family. He was created by God for the sake of humanity who needed him for their welfare.

As Guru Nanak considered himself to be God's child, his family included humanity at large and not just his relatives. He had to fulfill his duty towards this larger family.

Guru Nanak's family did not want to stop him from something which was the divine will.

So they let him go to fulfill the wishes of his *Sat Kartar* which was to remove all evil from society, spread the message of love and happiness everywhere, and bring human beings close to God.

Guru Nanak warmly hugged his family members one by one and bade them farewell.

Mardana also bade farewell to his family members. He was now ready to leave with Guru Nanak.

Guru Nanak went away with Mardana to spread the word of God.

MILK AND BLOOD

Guru Nanak and Mardana went from place to place, spreading the message of love and peace, and singing the praises of God.

Guru Nanak would sing his own musical hymns to get his teachings across to the people.

Wherever he went, he used the language of that area, so that common people could understand his teachings.

He travelled over the whole of India and even deep into the east, west and north.

When they reached Saidpur, they stayed in the hut of a poor carpenter named Lalo.

The rich people did not like the fact that a saint was living in the house of a person belonging to a low caste. But Guru Nanak continued to stay with the poor Lalo in his hut.

Guru Nanak

Guru Nanak preferred to live in a poor but honest man's hut rather than in the luxurious house of a rich landlord.

The Chief of the place, Malik Bhago, felt very bad that Guru Nanak had not come to his house for a meal when he had invited him.

He asked Guru Nanak, "Why did you refuse to come to my house to have a meal? Why are you staying in the hut of this poor carpenter? Why aren't you staying in the house of somebody who is rich and can provide you with comfort and luxury?"

In reply Guru Nanak said, "Get me some sweets from your house."

Malik Bhago asked his servants to get some sweets from his house.

Guru Nanak told Lalo, "Lalo, get me a piece of bread from your house."

Lalo went and brought a piece of bread from his house.

In one hand, Guru Nanak held a piece of dry bread from the poor man's hut and in the other, he held a piece of sweet from the rich man's house.

Then he tightly squeezed both his fists, with the sweet and the bread in it.

Drops of milk fell from the poor man's bread, but drops of blood fell from the rich man's sweet.

Nanak then explained to Malik Bhago, "You earn money by cheating the poor. That is why blood came out from the sweet. But this poor man has worked hard himself. That is why drops of milk came out from his dry bread."

Nanak further said, "I have chosen to stay with Lalo because he is an honest and hard working man. So what if he is poor?"

The rich man felt very sorry about the kind of life he had lead. He felt ashamed that he had made money by cheating the poor.

He replied, "I will give all my money to the poor, and I will look after them throughout my life."

Nanak blessed him and told him, "Malik Bhago, the Lord cherishes those who lead a truthful and honest life."

A lesson that we should learn from this true story is that one should work hard and earn by honest means.

Guru Nanak taught people to live a life of honesty and hard work.

After their stay in Saidpur, Nanak and Mardana continued with their travels, singing the praises of God.

Once they stayed on the outskirts of a city. It was a rainy season yet many people came to meet Guru Nanak.

There was one follower who came regularly, but later he got attracted to a dancing girl. After that he would leave his house saying that he was going to listen to the sermons of Guru Nanak, but would actually go to the dancer's house.

There was a friend of his who regularly came to meet Guru Nanak.

One day when he was on his way to meet Guru Nanak, this friend got pricked by a thorn. However, the other man got a gold coin when he was on his way to meet the dancing girl.

The friend asked Guru Nanak how fair was this that when he was on his way to do something good , he was pricked by a thorn, while the other friend who was going to meet a dancing girl got rewarded by getting a gold coin.

Guru Nanak explained, "The fact is that your friend was supposed to get a lot of money but because he did the wrong thing, he got only one gold coin."

Guru Nanak

The other friend asked, "But why did I get pricked by a thorn? I come here regularly, and I try to follow the path of righteousness."

"You were supposed to be punished very badly for some bad deed you did in your previous birth. But because you are being good, you just got the prick of a thorn as a punishment," answered Guru Nanak.

The friend then understood that being good was the correct thing to do. Those who commit bad deeds would be punished sooner or later. He started believing that whatever happens, happens for the best.

He continued coming to listen to Guru Nanak's sermons till he and Mardana moved on from there and went to Kurukshetra.

Guru Nanak roamed in the northern part of India and reached Haridwar.

QUESTIONING OF MEANINGLESS CUSTOMS

Guru Nanak and Mardana went to the holy city of Haridwar to bathe in the holy river Ganga.

There Guru Nanak saw a number of pilgrims offering water to the sun in the sky.

Guru Nanak asked the pilgrims, "What are you doing?"

One pilgrim replied, "We are giving water to the sun for the souls of our forefathers, who have died."

Guru Nanak turned around and started throwing water in the opposite side.

The pilgrim asked, "What are you doing?"

"I am throwing water for my fields in Punjab," answered Guru Nanak.

"You are really foolish. How can you water your fields from here. They are so far away," said the pilgrim.

Guru Nanak replied, "If the water you throw from here can reach the sun, it can surely reach my dry lands in Punjab, which are only some hundred miles away."

All the people who were having bath in the Ganga recognised the truth of what he was saying.

Guru Nanak's words made people re-think about an old custom that had no meaning.

NANAK MATA

After Haridwar, Guru Nanak and Mardana took the route towards Gorakh Mata, where the devotees of Guru Gorakhnath lived.

Guru Nanak and Mardana reached there during the winter months. Mardana asked the yogis, sitting around a fire, if they could give him some fire to keep warm.

Initially, the yogis of the Gorakh Mata behaved scornfully towards Guru Nanak.

So when Mardana asked them for fire, the yogis taunted him by saying, "Why don't you ask your Guru for fire?"

Seeing Mardana's discomfort, Guru Nanak ignited a pile of firewood merely by looking at it. Mardana could now enjoy the fire and keep warm.

All of a sudden, the weather changed and it began to rain. As a result, the fire that was lit by the yogis got extinguished.

Guru Nanak

However, the fire that was lit by Guru Nanak remained unaffected and continued to burn as before.

Seeing this, the yogis realised their mistake and bowed before him.

The next day, the yogis of the Gorakh Mata came to Guru Nanak for a religious discussion.

Guru Nanak told them, "Brothers, this life of seclusion and renunciation, where one cannot offer one's services to our fellow human beings, is worthless."

He told them that one should live an honest and truthful life of a God-oriented man of the world.

He also told them that true religion was not a matter of a specific garb or visiting pilgrimages. One can find the way to true religion only when one looks on all men as equal and remains pure and honest.

The impact of Guru Nanak's teachings on them can be seen from the fact that 'Gorakh Mata' became 'Nanak Mata'.

SPREADING THE WORD OF GOD

Guru Nanak travelled far towards the east of India. Wherever he and Mardana went, they would sit under a tree, sing devotional songs and preach people about God's word.

In the holy words of Guru Nanak was the message of human love and equality.

This was a much needed message at that time because of the growing religious intolerance between the Hindus and the Muslims.

In Guru Nanak's teachings, we find the best of both the religions, Hinduism and Islam.

He tried to unite both in this way. He took the belief in one God from the Muslims. He inculcated the karma theory from Hindus in which the reward or punishment depends on the type of action a person does.

Above all Guru Nanak wanted that people should take up the path of righteousness in their lives.

He was concerned with man and his fate. He told men that God was for every person.

In those times, caste system was followed very strictly. People were considered of high or low birth based on the family they were born into.

Guru Nanak

The *Brahmins* occupied the highest position in the social ladder. They were learned men who were responsible for imparting education and conducting all kinds of religious ceremonies.

The *Kshatriyas* were next. They were the ruling class, who excelled in military skills.

The *Vaishyas* were traders and merchants who dealt in money matters.

The *Sudras* were the people who served the three high ranking castes. They were considered as low caste people and were treated as untouchables. They laboured as sweepers and cleaners, doing all menial jobs.

The higher castes considered themselves above the Sudras and ill-treated them.

Guru Nanak taught people that everyone was equal and there was no high or low caste.

In a society, where the Hindu community was internally divided into castes and where there was a growing hatred among the Hindus and the Muslims, Guru Nanak's message of equality was much needed.

Guru Nanak voiced against the injustice done to the Sudras, who were ill-treated by the people of other castes and were not even allowed to enter the temples.

They were humiliated and were called 'untouchables'. No one wanted to touch them or let them come inside their houses. Even looking at them was considered inauspicious.

They had to live in poverty on the outskirts of the city or village.

When Guru Nanak told the so called 'low' people that they were equal to the others, he not only gave them happiness but also rescued them from a sense of inferiority which they had internalized because for years they had been told that they were lower and inferior to others.

Guru Nanak taught that even those who were considered as 'low' by society could remember God and worship the Almighty like the so called 'high' people.

Guru Nanak said that as all people had a common God, they were all brothers and sisters. He said that for God all men were equal as they were all His children.

His teachings brought about a feeling of happiness to the Sudras.

Though Guru Nanak's message of equality found much favour among the poor and downtrodden masses, the high caste people did not like it. They were not ready to mix with the low caste people.

So Guru Nanak had many people who were against him because of his teachings, but he never hated his enemies.

For him the real enemies were not those who disliked him personally but those who were the enemies of humanity at large. Like the cruel rulers who hurt people or those who cheated the poor.

He did not like dishonest people or thieves who stole from others.

He preached his people to follow thoughts and actions that were honest and morally good. He wanted to turn people on the path towards God.

He told the people to stop following all that was evil and dishonest.

At times when he was preaching, his enemies would come and create problems.

Some of them would throw tomatoes, shoes and rotten things at Guru Nanak, but he did not move from the path of righteousness. He would still preach that all men were equal as they were all God's children.

The things that were thrown at him fell on him as flowers, and everyone would shout *Sat Shree Akal*. His enemies were always fewer than his followers.

GOD IS OURS

Along with Guru Nanak, thinkers such as Surdas and Kabir preached that the Hindus and the Muslims were equal. These great men spread reformist ideas in the Indian society.

To consolidate their power and upper caste position, the *Brahmins* made such customs and rituals which the common people could not understand.

The poor people had to pay a lot to the priests for the religious customs because of which they incurred huge debts.

The power and the position of the *Brahmins* had so far been unquestioned.

Guru Nanak wanted that people should not follow these useless customs, but should simply believe in God.

He said many things that amazed people to no end. He told them that one is a Sudra or a Brahmin not by birth but by *karma* or deeds.

He also told them that they need not follow the obsolete customs and rituals to come closer to the Almighty but simply devote themselves to God with a sincere heart.

So far the priests had taught the people that they could reach God only through complicated rites and rituals which only the priests could perform. But now Nanak told them that anyone could be near God simply by chanting his name with a sincere heart.

This was surprisingly new for the people as for many years they had been told that they couldn't worship God. They were even forbidden to touch the wells of the high caste people because they were considered 'low' in body and in soul.

Now they were being told by Guru Nanak that they were as good as the priests. They could reach God just like the other people who were of a higher caste. Thus, the priests felt that their position was threatened by such messages of equality.

The teachings of Guru Nanak were important as they changed the thinking of many men.

After twelve years, Guru Nanak came back and then he started for his second journey.

He travelled south as far as Sri Lanka. On his return he stopped at Kartarpur.

Then he began his missionary tours again to spread God's message. On his third great journey he went right up to Tibet.

Wherever Nanak went, he would wear robes which were a mixture of Hindu and Muslim wear.

When people asked him whether he was a Hindu or a Muslim, he always replied, "I am a man of God."

When he went on his fourth great journey towards the north-west India, he wore the blue clothes of a Muslim pilgrim.

Then he visited Mecca, Medina and Baghdad.

The four missionary tours he took to spread the word of God are called the *Char Udasis*.

GOD IS EVERYWHERE

When Guru Nanak reached Mecca, the holy city of the Muslims, he and Mardana lay down to rest near the Kabba.

The Qazi came and shouted at Guru Nanak, "How dare you sleep with your feet pointing towards the holy Kaaba!"

Guru Nanak replied, "I am a man of God. For me God is everywhere."

He requested the Qazi, "Turn my feet in the direction where there is no Kaaba."

The *Qazi* turned around and was amazed to see the Kaaba on all sides. He did not know what to say because wherever he turned he saw the Kaaba. Now he realised that God is everywhere.

He honestly admitted to the truth of Guru Nanak's words that there is no place where God is not present. He fell at his feet asking forgiveness.

KODEY'S SPIRITUAL REBIRTH

Once when Guru Nanak and Mardana were going through a forest, Mardana volunteered, "I will get something to eat."

A terrible demon-like man caught Mardana. His name was Kodey, and he was a cannibal who ate human beings.

Kodey caught Mardana and put him in a huge vessel of boiling oil. Mardana at once thought of Guru Nanak. When he meditated on Guru Nanak's name, the boiling oil did not hurt him. It seemed as if the oil was cold.

Knowing his companion and follower to be in trouble, Guru Nanak started looking for him. He reached the place where Kodey had kept Mardana.

Guru Nanak spoke to Kodey, "We are human beings and it is wrong to eat each other."

He further said, "Life is a gift from God. We must thank Him for it and chant his name. The path you have taken will

Guru Nanak

lead you to the burning fire of hell."

Guru Nanak went on talking to Kodey who got convinced with his ideas. Such was Nanak's power of persuasion and the aura of his personality that Kodey folded his hands and asked forgiveness. He promised that he would never kill humans again.

Guru Nanak had a lot of effect on the people he spoke to. He could convince people easily and effectively, such was the greatness of his mind and the impact of his charismatic personality. He had the ability to touch everyone's heart and impress them.

Wherever he went, he gained many followers. He seemed a prophet to the people because he seemed to be endowed with superhuman powers as he could read their innermost thoughts.

PANJA SAHIB

In 1520, Guru Nanak went to the North-West Frontier province.

Guru Nanak decided to stay there. He sat under a Peepul tree of a valley. A Muslim saint named Vali Kandhari lived on the top of the hill.

Mardana would go to the top of the hill and get water. But one day Vali didn't let Mardana take water from the spring and said, "Why don't you ask your Guru for water?"

In a miserable state, Mardana came to Guru Nanak and told him that Vali was not letting him take water.

Guru Nanak said, "Mardana, chant the name of the Almighty." Soon the spring on the top of the hill dried up, and a spring came out in the valley near where Guru Nanak was staying.

Seeing this, the Muslim saint got very angry and pushed a big boulder at Guru Nanak.

Guru Nanak stopped the huge boulder with the open palm of his hand.

Even today there is a shrine with the name of *Panja Sahib* which has a huge boulder with the imprint of Guru Nanak's hand.

Guru Nanak and Mardana came back to India in 1521.

Guru Nanak wanted to meet Lalo, so he went to his city. When he reached the city, he saw that it had been destroyed by a military attack.

Guru Nanak had told Lalo during his last visit to go away from that city, as it would be attacked by Babur.

Guru Nanak saw that many mutilated bodies were lying around, women were crying and houses were completely destroyed. This spectacle of devastation caused much pain to him.

Mardana stopped a man and asked, "What has happened here? What is the cause of this mass destruction? Who has killed so many people?"

The man replied, "The Mughal Emperor Babur attacked our city. He gave orders to kill all the people, even those who were unarmed."

Mardana asked, "Many people must have died. But all of them could not have been guilty. Why were innocent people killed?"

Guru Nanak answered, "Wait under this banyan tree. I will come and give you the answer to your question."

While Mardana was sitting under the tree, an ant bit him. In his anger at being bitten, he killed many ants under his feet.

Then Nanak came and said, "Now, Mardana, do you understand how innocent people get killed along with the guilty?"

Mardana said, "Yes, I now undertand."

When Guru Nanak denounced this barbarous act of Babur in strong words, Mughal soldiers came and arrested him and Mardana.

They were put in a prison where a number of people were imprisoned. All the prisoners had to grind grains using heavy stone grinders. Many old people found it very difficult to do this.

On seeing such suffering, Guru Nanak felt extremely sad. He started singing a song about the suffering of those people.

Babur heard the sad song and exclaimed, "This voice touches my heart! Bring the singer to me."

When Guru Nanak was taken to Babur, he asked him about what he had been singing.

Guru Nanak replied, "I sang to God to come and see the pain which was being given to His people."

Babur felt very bad as Guru Nanak made him realise that he had hurt people and was the cause of their sufferings.

Babur admitted, "I have done much wrong. What can I do now to make up?"

Guru Nanak suggested, "Let the prisoners go free and give their lands back to them."

Babur listened to what Nanak said, and then he gave orders to set the prisoners free.

Then he said to Guru Nanak, "Holy man, I have obeyed you. The prisoners have been set free. Tell me, will I ever become the Emperor of India?"

Guru Nanak replied, "Yes, you will become the Emperor of India. But you should remember to be a just ruler."

He continued, "You should take care of your people because that is the duty of every good ruler. Instead of killing and exploiting them, you should win the hearts of the people."

Babur promised that he would take good care of his people.

Guru Nanak's holy words impressed Babur, and he told his soldiers to free Guru Nanak and Mardana.

Guru Nanak

Guru Nanak's words came true, as Babur did become the Emperor of India after sometime.

After the missionary tours, Guru Nanak came back to India to practice what he had preached.

He wanted to practice his teachings while living in a household rather than living a life of an ascetic or a traveller.

He had called his family to stay with him. His wife Sulakhni and his two sons came to live with him in Kartarpur. The family was reunited.

There he started a common kitchen or *langar* where everyone could come and eat. It did not matter whether the people were rich or poor, of a low caste or a high caste. They all sat together and ate the food cooked in the same kitchen.

Even today the Sikhs follow this custom of *langar* in their holy shrines called *Gurudwaras*. These are open kitchens where all who come have to eat the same food sitting together at the same place.

Guru Nanak tried to remove the artificial divides constructed by men by making people of different caste, class and gender sit and eat together.

He also opened *Dharamshalas* or *Manjis* which became meeting places for Sikhs to meditate and spread the word of God.

In the morning, the *Japji* was sung. In the evening, the *Sodar* and the *Aarti* were sung.

His followers would sit and listen to him and sing hymns with him.

His name spread far and wide, and his followers increased in number.

Guru Nanak

All the offerings that the people gave to him were given to the poor. He himself supervised the food and offerings that were given to the poor.

As Guru Nanak spread his message in the language of common people, i.e. Punjabi, the people felt close to Sikhism.

He preached in favour of brotherhood, love and faith in only one God. And he preached against formal ritualism, idol worship and asceticism.

He preached that people should practice a disciplined worldly life instead of rejecting worldly life altogether.

LEHNA

In 1532, Guru Nanak was working in his fields when a person came to meet him. He was Lehna Singh.

Lehna Singh was born in 1504 in the village of Harike in Ferozepur district in Punjab.

He was the son of a trader named Pheru. His mother's name was Mata Ramo.

Lehna was born in a Hindu family and was a devout worshipper of Goddess Durga.

Once when he heard a recitation of Guru Nanak's hymn, he felt his mind captured by it. It was then that he decided to go and visit Guru Nanak in Kartarpur.

On meeting Guru Nanak, he became his loyal and faithful disciple. He devoted himself to the service of Guru Nanak and his followers.

Once Guru Nanak had tied a few bundles of grass for the cattle. When he asked his two sons to carry these bundles home, they refused saying that it was not befitting the sons of the Guru to do such menial work.

The work that Guru Nanak's sons refused to do was gladly accepted by Lehna.

As he carried those bundles of wet and muddy grass, drops of muddy water fell on his fine silk clothes. But this did not bother him; he was too happy to get this chance to serve Guru Nanak.

Guru Nanak wanted to appoint someone who would carry on the spiritual message after him. Once, to test his followers, he said, "My bowl has fallen into the sewer drain."

Without waiting for a second, Lehna went and took out the bowl.

Once Nanak was going with Lehna and his two sons. They saw what seemed to be a dead body with a sheet covering it.

"Go and eat it," said Nanak.

His sons refused to eat it, but Lehna agreed to eat it. As he removed the cover, he found a tray full of food.

Lehna first served it to Guru Nanak and then to others.

Guru Nanak blessed him for being an ideal disciple and a true Sikh.

Guru Nanak's wife wanted one of their sons to be named the successor. But Guru Nanak wanted to choose a successor only on merit.

Lehna was an ideal student. He loved to obey and serve Guru Nanak. He found true happiness in doing all that Guru Nanak wished him to do.

He recited Guru Nanak's hymns and chanted God's name with a sincere heart and true faith.

So Lehna was chosen by Guru Nanak as his successor to carry on the spiritual message.

Guru Nanak

The ceremony of appointing Lehna as the successor took place.

Guru Nanak called him his own image, a part of his *ang*. So he gave Lehna the new name of Angad, Guru Angad.

Guru Nanak had a very simple ceremony for making Guru Angad the successor. He put five coins and a coconut in front of him and said, "You are my own image."

Guru Nanak bowed before Guru Angad, and he asked Bhai Buddha to put a saffron mark on the forehead of Guru Angad.

When they went for prayers, Guru Nanak made Guru Angad sit on his seat of the *guru* or teacher.

In this way, Guru Angad became the successor of Guru Nanak. This choosing of a successor showed how well Guru Nanak had thought out things.

He had planned that even after him, the faith he had started would be continued. There would be a guru to guide the followers.

The common kitchen would be continued in the *Gurudwaras*, and this would help to establish a sense of equality among the people.

When they got together to eat, they would also sing hymns and chant God's name.

Guru Nanak was in deep thought and meditation for sometime after appointing his successor.

He felt that he had done the work that God had given him to do.

He had travelled and preached the word of God for twenty-five years.

He had composed hymns that had answers to the problems of religion and society.

He had studied Islam, Hinduism, Jainism and Buddhism, and had tried to understand the best in them.

He had started a new religion called *Sikhism*. He had preached well and then practiced what he had preached.

His followers saw him meditating and felt that Guru Nanak's end was near.

The Hindus said, "We will cremate Guru ji."

The Muslims said, "We will bury Guru ji."

Soon the Hindus and the Muslims started fighting over this issue. Seeing them fight among each other, Guru Nanak felt pained. He did not want people to fight over him, as all through his life he had spread the message of brotherhood.

He asked them to stop fighting and said, "Place flowers on either side of me. Hindus may put them on the right and Muslims on the left. Those whose flowers remain fresh tomorrow can do what they want with me."

He then asked his followers to pray. He lay down covering himself with a sheet at night.

In the early hours of 22nd September, 1539, Guru Nanak Dev ji gave up his body. He was now united with God, his *Sat Kartar*, forever.

When the followers removed the sheet in the morning, there was only a heap of fresh flowers.

As all the flowers were fresh, they understood that Guru Nanak was of no caste; he was neither a Hindu nor a Muslim.

The Muslims took the flowers and buried them, while the Hindus cremated the flowers.

Probably Guru Nanak did this to teach his followers that they should not have fought.

If they had understood the true teachings of Nanak, they would have understood that he wanted unity and that he was neither a Hindu nor a Muslim.

He had always taught people to unite in the spirit of brotherhood and believe in one God. His death was a true picture of what he had always tried to preach.

MARDANA

ardana was Guru Nanak's Muslim follower and friend, who accompanied him throughout his missionary tours in India and abroad.

He was born in 1459 in the village of Rai Bhoe of Talwandi, now in Pakistan. He was ten years older than Guru Nanak.

He was the son of a *Mirasi* couple. *Mirasis* were ministrels who recorded a family's history in the form of long poems.

His father's name was Badra and his mother's name was Lakhi. Mardana's mother had six children, all of whom died during birth. She named the seventh child Marjana, meaning the one who dies.

But Guru Nanak starting calling him Mardana, meaning the one who wouldn't die.

Wherever they went, Guru Nanak would sing devotional songs and Mardana would accompany him by playing on his musical instrument, rubab.

Mardana was not only an exceptionally good rubab player, but also a poet of some merit. One of his *slokas* appears in the Guru Granth Sahib.

There are two versions of his death. One says that he died in 1534, in Kartarpur when he seriously fell ill with no hope of recovery. He was born in a Muslim household, but he left it to Guru Nanak's will to dispose his body.

Guru Nanak asked him if he wished a tomb to be made for him to make him famous in the world.

He replied, "If the *Sat Kartar* is freeing me from this bodily prison why would I want to entomb myself in stone."

When Mardana gave up his body to return to his heavenly home, Guru Nanak consigned his body to the River Ravi.

The other version of his death says that he died in Baghdad. After making a pilgrimage to the holy shrines of Mecca and Medina, Mardana felt increasingly tired and exhausted. He considered himself to be lucky to die at this holy place.

THE TEN GURUS

The ten Sikh *gurus* or teachers are:

1. GURU NANAK DEV JI
   1469-1539
2. GURU ANGAD DEV JI
   1539-1552
3. GURU AMARDAS JI
   1552-1574
4. GURU RAM DAS JI
   1574-1581
5. GURU ARJAN DEV JI
   1581-1606
6. GURU HARGOBIND JI
   1606-1644
7. GURU HAR RAI JI
   1644-1661
8. GURU HARKRISHAN JI
   1661-1664
9. GURU TEGH BAHADUR JI
   1665-1675
10. GURU GOBIND SINGH JI
    1675-1708

Guru Nanak

Some gurus played a very important part in the politics of India.

When the tenth guru, Guru Gobind Singh was asked who would be the guru after him, he declared that the eleventh Sikh guru would be the 'Guru Granth Sahib'.

He did the ceremony that was done to appoint a guru by placing a coconut and five coins in front of the holy book. He proclaimed it as the Sikh Guru for all times to come.

SIKHISM

Guru Nanak, the founder of Sikhism, crucially changed the way people thought.

What Guru Nanak started is still being followed by *Sikhs* (meaning disciple) or *Sardars* all over the world.

A Guru's Sikh is supposed to carry these five things beginning with the letter *k*, that is, *kesh* (hair), *kirpan* (dagger), *kachha* (lower underclothes), *kara* (steel bangle) and *kangha* (comb).

Sikhism, in the beginning, believed in peace, but after the severe torture that Guru Arjan Dev ji had to undergo at the hands of Jahangir and at the cruel execution of the ninth Sikh guru, Guru Tegh Bahadur, the Sikhs decided to train themselves in the skills of warfare. This was done to fight against injustice and tyranny.

The Sikhs have proved to be one of the bravest fighting groups of India. This is evident in the fights they fought against the Mughals .

Guru Nanak

THE ELEVENTH GURU

The Guru Granth Sahib ji has many hymns and religious songs composed by Guru Nanak Dev ji. Guru Arjan Dev ji compiled it, and the rest of the gurus added to it. But they all kept the name of Nanak in the hymns.

The Guru Granth Sahib has 1430 pages in poetry form.

It has the verses of Guru Nanak, which he sang in the language *Gurumukhi*.

All the beliefs and faiths of Sikhs come from these religious songs composed by the ten gurus.

Verses of other saints and poets have also been included in the Guru Granth Sahib. They have been included as they prove the basic teachings of Sikhism.

The Sikh gurus didn't believe in idol worship. So there is no idol worship in Sikhism. The sacred book, Guru Granth Sahib, is now worshipped by the Sikhs.

The Guru Granth Sahib is kept in *Gurudwaras* where the Sikhs come and worship it.

The Sikhs worship the book and sing praises of God as Guru Nanak used to sing.

The followers sing holy words of their gurus called *gurubani* wherein they pay homage to God.

There is the common kitchen called *langar* in all *Gurudwaras*.

Primary importance is given to the Guru Granth Sahib on every festival of the Sikhs. This shows that the moral teachings are at the centre of their faith.

The religious celebration of the Sikhs is called *Gurupurab*.

The Sikhs believe that the guru is there as a guide to explain, how one should live one's life. The guru said that the morality of being good and removing evil is necessary.

The Guru Granth Sahib reminds the Sikhs of the rules that Guru Nanak had laid by leading a life based on simple living and high thinking.

After twenty-five years of travelling, Guru Nanak settled in Kartarpur because he wanted to spread his message among the masses.

He went to different parts of India and the neighbouring countries, and left *Dharamshalas* so that his followers could meet and meditate on God.

Gurudwaras are found all over the world and the common kitchens help travellers and poor people.

The weddings of the Sikhs take place in the *Gurudwaras*. The couple takes four rounds of the holy book.

Guru Nanak had such a far reaching effect that his teachings are found to have relevance even today.

This is because what the people need today is to be good, hard-working and honest.

The modern world of today, in spite of many advancements, has forgotten the truths of brotherhood and love. Moral values are lost and man has become self-centered and materialistic. If only we could follow the teachings of the great gurus, it would be the greatest tribute to them.